High Win] Day Trading Setups

High Win Rate Day Trading Strategies for Trading Crypto and Forex in 2023

Copyright ©

All rights reserved. No part of this book may be reproduced, stored in a retrieval system, or transmitted in any form or by any means, electronic, mechanical, photocopying, recording, scanning, or otherwise, without the prior written permission of the publisher.

Disclaimer

This book is not to be used for financial advice.

All the material contained in this book is provided for informational purposes only. The author does not guarantee any results from the use of this information.

No responsibility can be taken for any results or outcomes resulting from the use of this material.

While every attempt has been made to provide information that is both accurate and effective, the author does not assume any responsibility for the accuracy or use/misuse of this information.

Table of Contents

1. Developing a Profitable Trading Strategy   2

2. Using Indicators to Find a Edge   5

3. High Win Rate Entry/Exit Signals Using Indicators   12

4. High Win Rate Day Trading Strategies   41

Getting Started

Creating a day trading strategy with a 70%+ win rate might sound impossible, but it's actually much easier then you think.

We will go into detail about what indicators can be used to create a strategy that yields a consistently high win rate and uncover the specific settings that work best.

You'll learn how to analyze the markets like an experienced trader, including techniques for spotting market tops/bottoms and identifying potential pumps before they take place.

The trading strategies in this book are mechanical rules based strategies that use the right combination of indicators to find high probability trade setups.

Let's get started!

1. Developing a Profitable Trading Strategy

To be successful, traders must employ sound strategy and risk management principles. Here we outline the basic elements of any profitable trading system:

Entries

Entries are the key to any successful trading system and involve determining when it is most advantageous to enter a position in the market.

Traders can use technical indicators such as moving averages, support/resistance levels or momentum oscillators to help determine when to get into a trade. When identifying entries, traders should also consider the overall market environment as well as their own risk tolerance.

Exits

Exits are just as important as entries and should be planned out before entering a position.

Traders can use technical indicators such as trend lines or price targets to identify potential exit points. A good exit signal will allow a trader to exit a position before price reverses while still maximizing their profits.

Traders can use set profit targets or set a trailing stop to help with exits. Trailing stops are especially useful because they can lock in profits while allowing the trader to stay in the trade if price continues to move in their favor.

Position Sizing

Position sizing is an important element of any trading system and refers to how much capital should be allocated to each position. Traders should consider their risk tolerance as well as the overall market environment when deciding how much to allocate to each position.

Position sizing also allows traders to control their exposure and limit any potential losses.

Risk Management

Risk management is critical for successful trading. This includes setting realistic profit targets and using protective stops that will limit losses if the market moves against the position.

Additionally, traders should watch for signs of market fatigue such as divergences, extreme overbought or oversold conditions and other price action clues that may signal an impending trend reversal.

By understanding and utilizing these key elements while creating a trading system, traders can increase their chances of success in the markets.

With careful study and practice, it is possible to develop a profitable trading strategy that is tailored to individual goals and objectives.

2. Using Indicators to Find a Edge

Indicators can be a valuable asset to traders of all experience levels. Indicators are mathematical calculations based on the price and/or volume of a security.

They are used by traders to help them identify potential trading opportunities and make decisions about when to enter or exit trades. There are dozens of different types of indicators, each with its own set of strengths and weaknesses. Experienced traders often use multiple indicators in combination to get a better overall view into the market's behavior.

However, beginners should start with one indicator at a time in order to get an understanding for how it works before attempting more complex strategies.

When using indicators, it is important for traders to understand how the indicator is calculated, its purpose, and what the signal it is providing means.

For example, a moving average can be used to identify potential trend reversals or support and resistance levels. On the other hand, relative strength index (RSI) can be used to identify overbought/oversold conditions in the market. Different indicators are suited to different trading styles and objectives.

Indicators can be broadly classified into two main types, mean reversion and trend following.

Mean Reversion Indicators

Mean reversion indicators are used to measure when an asset is trading above or below its historical average price (mean).

When price moves too far away from the mean, there is a high probability that it will reverse or pull back to the mean.

These strategies tend to work best in markets where prices move within a range, providing opportunities for scalping and day trading strategies.

Traders look for signals that indicate when price is too overextended from the mean by using indicators such as Bollinger Bands, Stochastics and Relative Strength Index.

Overbought/Oversold Signals

Mean reversion indicators typically use overbought/oversold signals to identify where price is likely to reverse. When an indicator is overbought, it indicates that the price has risen too quickly and is likely to pull back.

Conversely, when an indicator is oversold, it indicates that the price has fallen too quickly and may soon reverse trend.

The idea behind overbought/oversold conditions is that if price moves too quickly in one direction, there will not be enough buyers or sellers to support that move, leading to a reversal.

Trend Following Indicators

Trend followers are different from mean reversion traders in that they aim to capitalize on market trends rather than seeking out corrections or reversals.

These indicators are used to identify the direction of trends, while providing entry and exit signals when a trend is reversing or a new trend is beginning.

The best trend following indicators will allow you to get in a new trend as early as possible, keeping you in the trend as long as possible before it reverses.

Using Filters To Identify Trending/Sideways Markets

It is important for traders to understand that different market conditions demand different types of indicators and strategies. Markets can be either trending or moving sideways, and it is essential to know which indicator signals work best in each type of market.

Traders use filters like the Average Directional Index (ADX) to identify whether a market is trending or ranging. The ADX measures the strength of a trend, providing an indication when a trend has begun to reverse or move sideways.

Once a trader identifies which type of market they are in, they can then adjust their entry/exit signals accordingly using indicators designed specifically for that type of environment.

The ADX

The Average Directional Movement Index (ADX) is a technical indicator which measures the strength of trend and volatility. It can be used to identify ranging and trending markets, as well as to filter out stronger trends that are not suitable for mean reversion scalping strategies.

If the ADX value is below 30, it indicates a weak trend or a market that is moving sideways in a range.

When the ADX is below 30, this can indicate ideal conditions for scalpers as the market will likely be in a range, and not in a strong trend.

Example of the ADX below 30 indicating a ranging market

In conclusion, scalping can be a profitable form of trading under certain market conditions.

Make sure to pay attention to the overall trend and market activity when deciding if scalping is right for you. You should also consider the liquidity of the market before entering any trades as this can have an impact on your profits and losses.

Breakout/Consolidation Filter (TradingView indicator)

The Breakout/Consolidation Filter is easily one of the best indicators for identifying ranging/trending markets.

This is a free indicator found on TradingView that was created by the TradingView community.

To Find this Indicator:

- Open the indicator search box on TradingView

- Type **Breakout/Consolidation Filter [jwammo12]** in the indicator search box

How it Works

This indicator is similar to the ADX, using a single line that moves up or down based on how strong the current trend is.

- If this indicator is below 50, price is in a period of consolidation

- If this indicator is above 50, price is trending and not consolidating

This indicator includes a yellow line at the 50 level to make it easier to see these signals.

Example of the Breakout/Consolidation Filter under 50 indicating price is ranging

As you can see this indicator works very well for identifying ranges, breakouts of consolidation and trends.

When Using This Indicator for Scalping:

- Only enter trades if the Breakout/Consolidation Filter is **under 50.**

We will look at some profitable scalping strategies using this indicator later on in this book, this is one of my favorite indicators and I use it in many of my strategies.

3. High Win Rate Entry/Exit Signals Using Indicators

This chapter includes highly accurate entry/exit signals from indicators found on the charting platform TradingView.

These are free indicators that other traders have created and coded on TradingView. There are thousands of indicators on TradingView which other members have created, but these are the best indicators I have found and use in my scalping strategies.

Important – These indicators should be used in a complete scalping strategy and not by themselves. You should also backtest and papertrade these signals first before using them with real money!

To access these indicators on TradingView:

1. Make a TradingView account (TradingView.com), you can sign up for a free account if you don't want to pay.

2. Open up a chart on TradingView, and click on the "indicators" icon found at the top toolbar.

3. Then simply type in the indicator you are looking for in the search box.

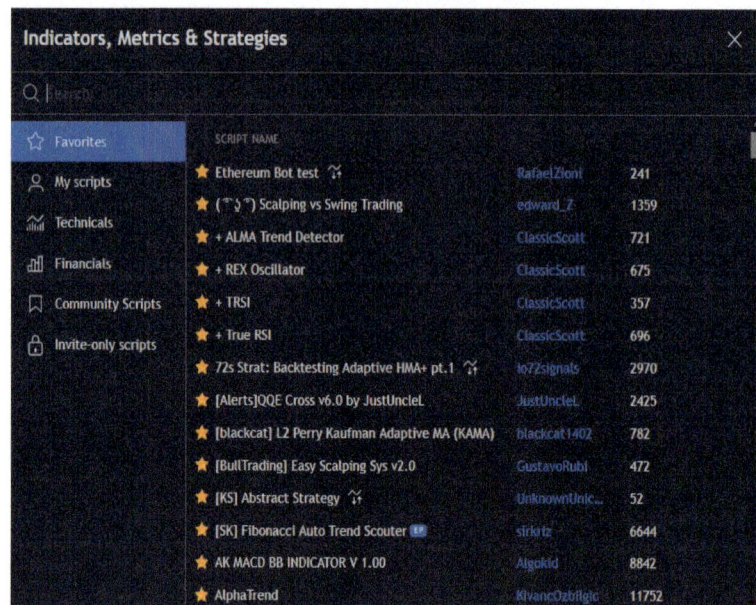

The TradingView indicator search box

Now that you know how to find these indicators, let's get started!

Indicator Entry/Exit #1: Bjorgum MTF MA
By: Bjorgum

To find this indicator, type "Bjorgum MTF MA" in the indicator search box on TradingView (by Bjorgum*)*

Overview:

This is indicator is a moving average that is extremely accurate at identifying trends and trend reversals early.

Signals occur when price crosses and closes above or below the moving average, with candles also changing color when a signal occurs. This indicator will keep you in trends for as long as possible with few false signals.

When using this indicator the color of the candles will change depending on the trend, with blue indicating a uptrend and red for a downtrend.

You can change the MA type in the indicator settings to better fit your style of trading. Avoid using this indicator in sideways markets with low volatility, since more false signals will occur in these conditions.

Indicator Tip:

- The DEMA and HMA are better for scalping, while the EMA and SMA are better for trading trends.

Long Entry:
- A candle crosses and closes above the MA
- The MA line color change from red to blue
- Candle color changes from red to blue

Long Exit:
- The MA color changes from blue to red
- A candle closes below the MA
- Candle color changes from blue to red (less reliable)

Example of entry and exit signals using the Bjorgum MTF MA

Short Entry:
- A candle crosses and closes below the MA
- The MA line change from blue to red
- Candle color changes from blue to red

Short Exit:
- The MA color changes from red to blue
- Candle color changes from red to blue (less reliable)

Indicator Entry/Exit #2: L2 KDJ with Whale Pump Detector

By: blackcat1402

To find this indicator, type "L2 KDJ with Whale Pump Detector" in the indicator search box on TradingView (by blackcat1402)

Overview:

This indicator is a variation of the KDJ indicators, which a momentum oscillator similar to the stochastic oscillator. It uses the K and D lines from the stochastic, but also uses another line called the J line – hence the name KDJ.

Signals are generated when all three lines cross over in a certain direction. The KDJ also includes overbought (above 100) and oversold (below 0) zones that can be used for entry/exit signals.

The signals from the KDJ will be the most reliable is sideways market conditions.

Indicator Tip:

- In the settings, remove the background colors on the KDJ

Long Entry:
One of the following can be used-

- A green "B" label appears on the KDJ
- The three lines of the KDJ cross up

Long Exit:
One of the following can be used-

- A red "S" label appears on the KDJ
- All three lines cross down
- The KDJ crosses above 100 (overbought)

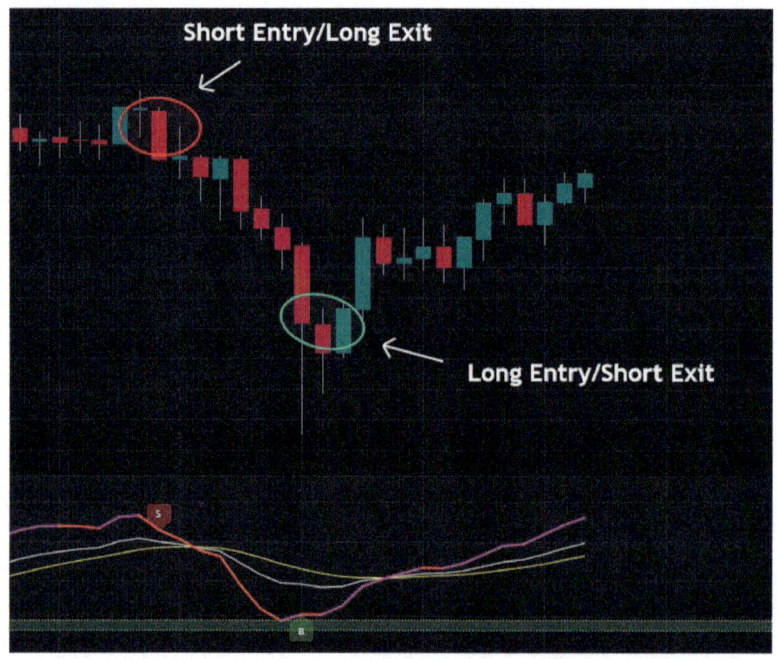

*Example of entry and exit signals using the L2 KDJ indicator*Short Entry:

One of the following can be used-

- A red "S" label appears on the KDJ
- The three lines of the KDJ cross down

Short Exit:
One of the following can be used-

- A green "B" label appears on the KDJ
- All three lines cross down
- The KDJ crosses below 20 (oversold)

Indicator Entry/Exit #3: ŠTD-Filtered, N-Pole Gaussian Filter [Loxx]

By Loxx

To find this indicator, type "STD-Filtered, N-Pole Gaussian Filter" in the indicator search box on TradingView (by Loxx)

Overview:

This is indicator is based on the Gaussian filter, which is similar a very smooth moving average that filters out noise. This indicator also uses filters that can be added on to avoid false signals.

The signals from this indicator are easy to identify and will change between green and red depending on trend direction.

Buy and sell arrows will also appear above/below bars.

Indicator Tip: In the settings, change the **Filter Options** to "Price" and set the **Filter Deviations** to 2.

Long Entry:
- Candle color changes to green
- A yellow arrow appears below a candle

Long Exit:
- Candle color changes to red
- A candle closes below the MA line
- A purple arrow appears above a candle

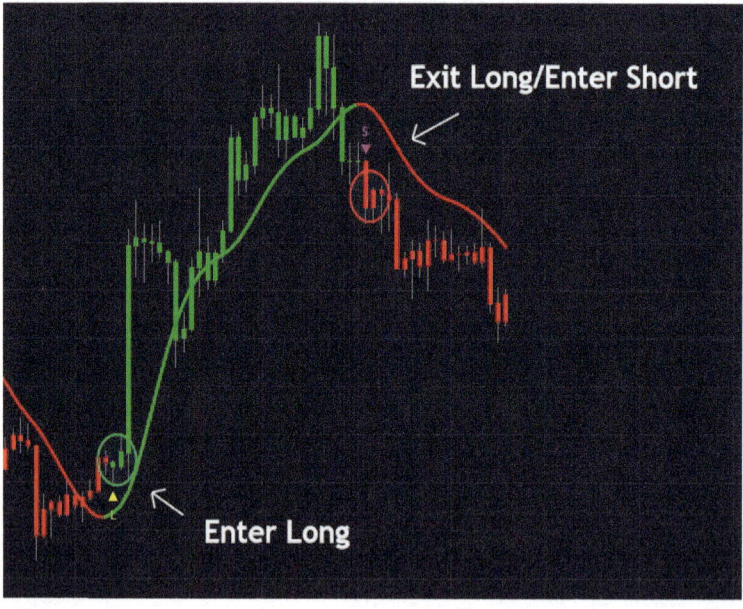

Example of a entry and exit signal using this indicator

Short Entry:
- Candle color changes to red
- A purple arrow appears above a candle

Short Exit:
- Candle color changes to green
- A candle closes above the MA line
- A yellow arrow appears above a candle

Indicator Entry/Exit #4: Trend Trigger Factor

By: everget

To find indicator, type "Trend Trigger Factor" in the indicator search box on TradingView (by everget)

Overview:

The Trend Trigger Factor (TTF) indicator is a oscillator similar to the RSI. The difference with the TTF compared to the RSI is that the overbought/oversold signals are more reliable and produces fewer false signals then the RSI.

How to use it:

Like with most overbought/oversold indicator signals, the TTF will provide the most accurate signals in sideways markets.

Once the OB/OS signal occurs it is important to wait for the TTF to cross out of overbought/oversold before using it as a valid signal.

Long Entry/Short Exit:
- The TTF crosses out of the oversold zone

Short Entry/Long Exit:
- The TTF crosses out of the overbought zone

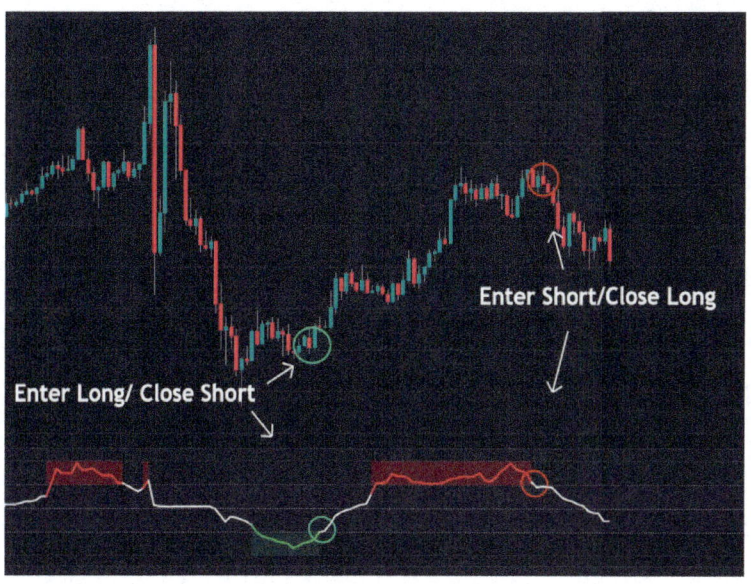

Example of Entry/Exit signals using the TTF indicator

Indicator Entry/Exit #5: Kaufman Moving Average Adaptive (KAMA)

By HPotter

To find this indicator, type "Kaufman Moving Average Adaptive" in the indicator search box on TradingView (by HPotter*)*

Overview:

The KAMA is a moving average that is designed to filter out non trending price movements and only follow price when a trend is occurring.

In a sideways market this moving average will appear flow and will only have a slope if price is trending. This reduces whipsaw signals that occur with other moving averages in non trending markets.

Long Entry:

- A candle crosses and closes above the KAMA
- The KAMA has a upward slope

Long Exit:

- A candle closes below the KAMA

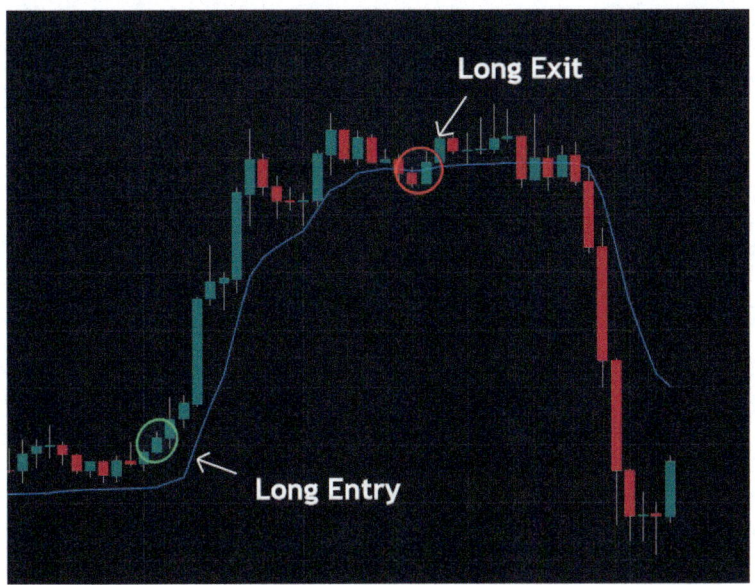

Long entry and exit signals using the KAMA

Short Entry:
- A candle crosses and closes below the KAMA
- The KAMA has a downward slope

Short Exit:
- A candle closes above the KAMA

Indicator Entry/Exit #6: HalfTrend Indicator
By: everget

To find indicator, type "halftrend" in the indicator search box on TradingView (by everget)

Overview:

The halftrend indicator is great for accurately predicting short term tops and bottoms in the market.

When a buy or sell signal occurs a arrow will appear below or above price making this a very simple to use and understand.

This indicator will work the best in markets with higher volatility, and larger price swings.

When volatility is very low this indicator will be less reliable, producing more false signals.

Note -In low volatility market conditions you may get better signals with the following settings:

- Amplitude 1
- Channel Deviation 1

Indicator tip – Turn off the ATR high/low boxes in the settings to make this indicator easier to see

Long Entry:
- Blue arrow appears below a candle
- The line changes to blue color

Long Exit:
Choose one of the following-
- red arrow appears above a candle
- The line changes to red color

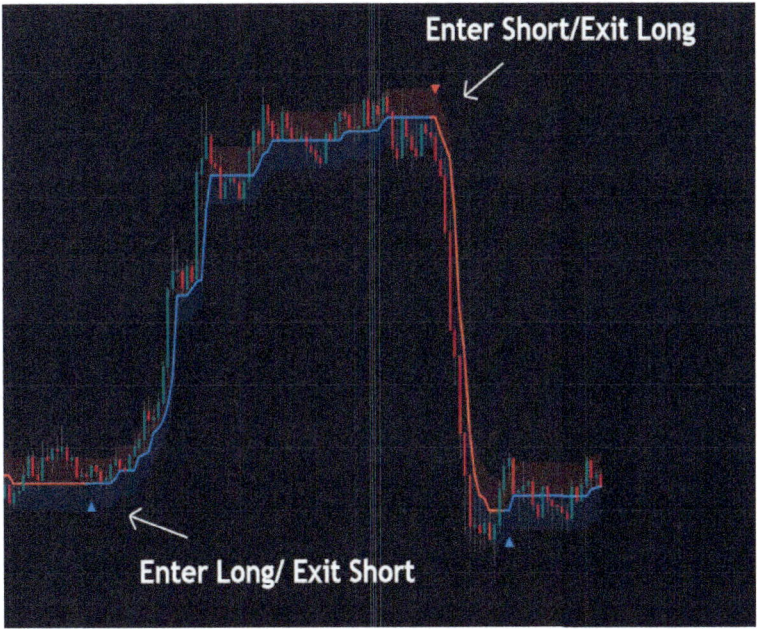

A screenshot of entry/exit signals using the halftrend indicator

Short Entry:
- Red arrow appears on top of a candle
- The line changes to red

Short Exit:
Choose one of the following-
- blue arrow appears below a candle
- The line changes to blue color

Indicator Entry/Exit #6: AlphaTrend

By: KivancOzbilgic

To find indicator, type "AlphaTrend" in the indicator search box on TradingView (by KivancOzbilgic*)*

Overview:

This indicator includes two lines based on the ATR (average true range) that will follow price similar to moving averages. Buy/sell signals will occur when these lines cross.

This indicator can accurately predict large price swings in the market without too many false signals.

This indicator is very easy to use, a "buy" or "sell" label will appear when the ATR lines cross and a signal occurs.

This indicator will work best in higher volatility where large price swings occur.

Avoid using this indicator if the volatility is too low, since it will produce false signals in these conditions.

Indicator Tip: You can change the colors of this indicator in the setting to make it easier to see

Long Entry:
- Price is above the AlphaTrend and a buy label appears

Long Exit:
- Price closes below the AlphaTrend
- A sell label appears

Example of Entry/Exit signals using the AphaTrend indicator

Short Entry:
- Price is below the AlphaTrend and a sell label appears

Short Exit:
- Price closes above the AlphaTrend
- A buy label appears

Indicator Entry/Exit #7: Angle Attack Follow Line Indicator

By Dreadblitz

To find indicator, type "Angle Attack Follow Line" in the indicator search box on TradingView (by Dreadblitz)

Overview:

The AAFLI is an ATR based indicator that also uses calculation from the Bollinger bands to generate buy and sell signals. This is one of my favorite trend following indicators and is extremely accurate at detecting trend changes in the market.

The AAFLI is displayed as a histogram at the bottom of the chart. When a signal occurs, candles will change between red and blue colors depending on the trend.

A buy/sell label will also appear on the histogram, making it very easy to identify signals on this indicator.

Indicator Tip:

In the settings –

- Turn off the background colors on the histogram
- Turn off all signals except the "buy" and "sell" signals

Long Entry:
- Candle color changes blue
- A "buy" label appears on the histogram

Long Exit:
- Candle color turns red and a "sell" label appears on histogram

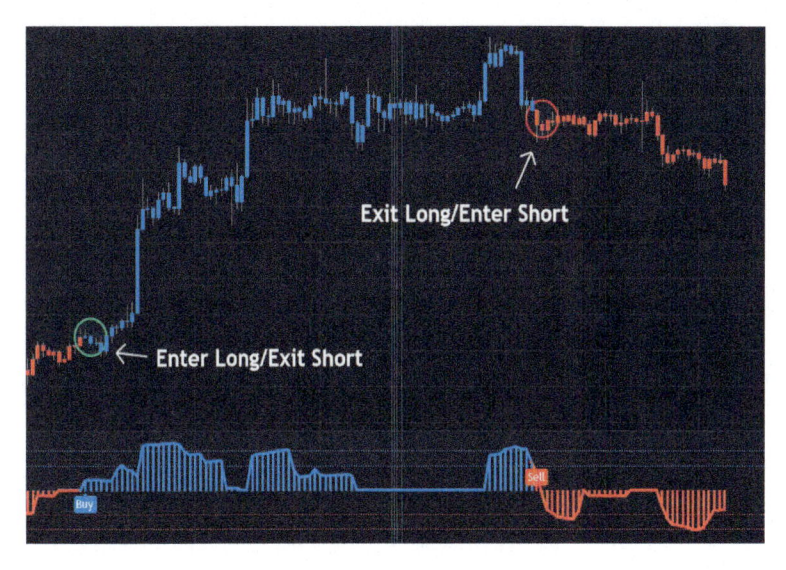

Example of entry/exit signals using the AAFLI indicator

Short Entry:
- Candle color changes red
- A "buy" label appears on the histogram

Short Exit:
- Candle color turns blue and a "buy" label appears on histogram

Indicator Entry/Exit #8: Reversal Finder
By: NS91

To find this indicator, type "reversal finder" in the indicator search box on TradingView (by NS91)

Overview:

The reversal finder indicator identifies false breaks of support/resistance levels to generate reversal signals. This indicator is very basic with single dots appearing above or below a candle when a signal occurs. This indicator produces highly accurate entry/exit signals when used in the right market conditions.

Note – The green and red dots are much stronger reversal signals then the yellow dots.

The reversal finder indicator will work the best in ranging/sideways markets. The signals from this indicator will be less reliable in strong trending markets.

For the best results, try using this indicator with a filter to avoid using this indicator in trending markets.

Indicator Tip: Change the range multiple to 2 for fewer false signals in the indicator settings

Long Entry/Short Exit:
- Green or dot appears below a candle

Short Entry/Long Exit:
- Red dot appears above a candle

Example of entry/exit signals using the reversal finder indicator

Indicator Entry/Exit #9: Zero Lag MACD Enhanced - Version 1.2

By: albert.callisto

To find indicator, type "Zero Lag MACD Enhanced - Version 1.2" in the indicator search box on TradingView (by albert.callisto*)*

Overview:

This is an improved and modified version of the commonly used MACD (moving average convergence divergence) indicator.

Like the regular MACD this version uses the MACD (fast) line and signal (slow) line to generate buy/sell signal. The signals produces from this version of the MACD are more accurate and has fewer false signals then the regular version.

This version also includes another EMA but its not needed and you can turn it off in the settings.

When using this indicator, it will work best in higher volatility price action and can reliably predict short term market tops and bottoms. When a crossover signal occurs a dot will appear on the indicator, making it easier to identify signals.

Indicator Tip:

To improve signal accuracy, change the following indicator setting -

- Fast MM period = 12
- Uncheck "Use EMA"
- Uncheck "Use Glaz algo"

Enter Long/Exit Short:
- The MACD line crosses above the signal line (green dot appears)

Enter Short/Exit Long:
- The MACD line crosses below the signal line (red dot appears)

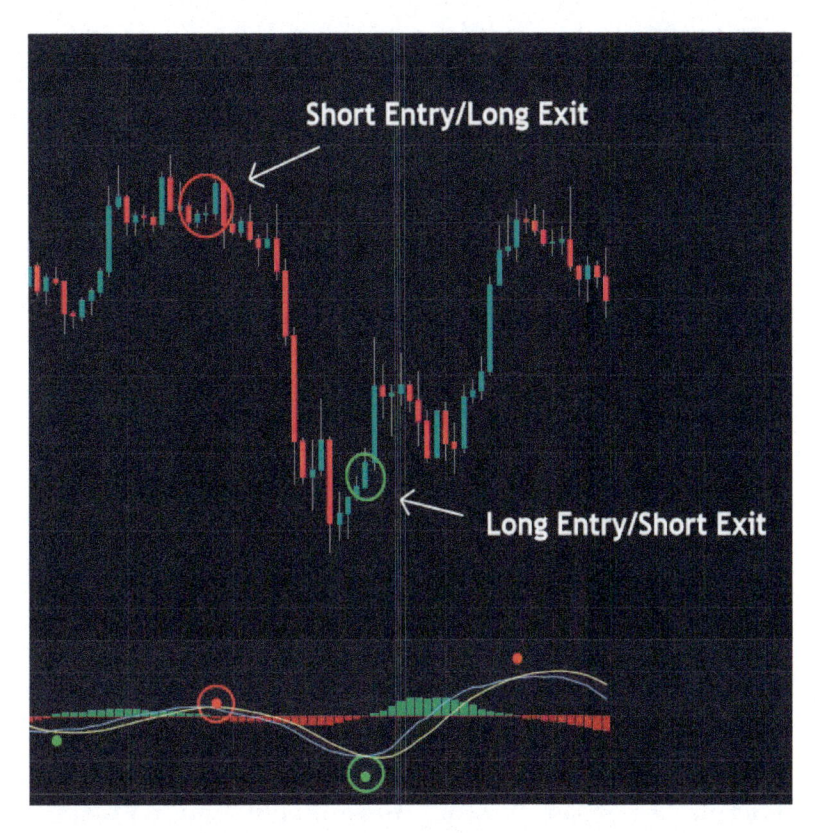

Example of Entry/Exit signals using the zero lag MACD enhanced indicator

4. High Win Rate Day Trading Strategies

Day trading is an exciting way to make money in the stock market. But while it can be a great source of income, it also has its risks. That's why it's important to find good setups for day trading that have a higher probability of leading to profits.

Five things to look for in a high probability setup

1. Volatility

Volatility refers to how much the price of an asset moves over a period of time - the more active and volatile an asset is, the more likely you will find trading opportunities within it. Look for assets with higher levels of volatility when searching for day trading setups.

2. Confluence of Signals

Confluence of signals refers to when two or more technical indicators generate a trade signal at the same time. If multiple indicators are pointing in the same direction, then this is an indication of strong momentum and a potentially profitable setup.

3. Momentum

Momentum is the rate of change in the price of an asset over time. Look for assets that show positive momentum when searching for good day trading setups as these tend to be more profitable than ones showing negative momentum.

4. Entry Signals In Direction of Trend

When looking for setups with a high win rate, you should always enter trades in the direction of the trend. This means that if the price is trending upwards, then your entry signal should be to buy. Conversely, if the price is trending downwards, then your signal should be to sell.

5. Risk/Reward Ratio

The risk/reward ratio refers to the amount of potential profit you can make compared to how much you could potentially lose. Whenever possible, look for setups with a favorable risk/reward ratio and always take into account your stop loss when placing trades.

By following these guidelines, you can find day trading setups that have a higher probability of leading to profits.

Now let's take a look at some high win rate trading strategies!

Strategy #1: Bollingerbands + UT Bot

Type of Strategy:

- Can be used for trend following or scalping

Strategy Overview:

This is a mean reversion strategy uses entry signals from the UT Bot indicator, and uses the Bollinger bands to filter out false signals from the UT Bot.

The UT bot is a ATR based indicator that can produce very accurate signals, but can also generate false signals from market noise. This strategy also uses the 200 SMA for trading in the overall trend direction.

The combination of these two indicators will provide highly profitable trades with few false signals.

Strategy Indicators:

- **Bollinger band** (default settings)
- **200 SMA** (simple moving average)
- **UT Bot Alert** (by QuantNomad)

Long Entry Conditions:

- Price is above the 200 SMA

- A candle is touching or below the bottom Bollinger band

- Enter when a candle color changes to green and a "buy" signal appears under candle

Long Exit Conditions:

Use one of the following-

- A candle touches the top Bollinger band (better for scalping)

- Candle color changes to red and a "sell" signal appears on top of candle (better for trend trading)

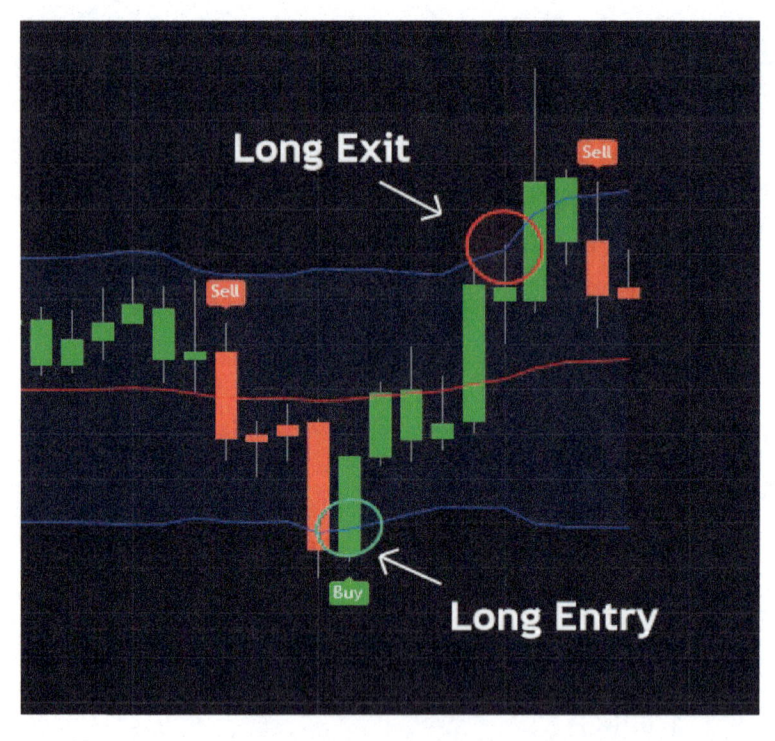

Long entry and exit for scalping using this strategy

Long entry and exit for trend trading using this strategy

Short Entry Conditions:
- Price is below the 200 SMA
- A candle is touching or above the top Bollinger band
- Enter when a candle color changes to red and a "sell" signal appears above candle

Short Exit Conditions:
Use one of the following-

- A candle touches the bottom Bollinger band (better for scalping)
- Candle color changes to green and a "buy" signal appears on top of candle (better for trend trading)

Strategy #2: HalfTrend Breakout Strategy

Type of Strategy:

- Trend following strategy

Strategy Overview:

This is a trend following strategy using the HalfTrend indicator for entries and exits.

The Breakout/Consolidation Filter indicator is used for avoiding entering trades in sideways market conditions, as many whipsaw (false) signals occur in these conditions.

The 200 SMA is also used to trade in the direction of the trend.

Strategy Indicators:

- **HalfTrend** (by everget)
- **Breakout/Consolidation Filter** (by jwammo12)
- **200 SMA**

Long Entry Conditions:
- Price is above the 200 SMA
- The Breakout /Consolidation Filter is above 50
- Enter when the HalfTrend turns blue and a blue arrow appears

Long Exit Conditions:
- The HalfTrend Line turns red
- A red arrow appears above a candle

Example of a long entry and exit using this strategy

Short Entry Conditions:
- Price is below the 200 SMA
- The Breakout /Consolidation Filter is above 50
- Enter when the HalfTrend turns red and a red arrow appears

Short Exit Conditions:
- The HalfTrend Line turns blue
- A blue arrow appears under a candle

Strategy #3: MFI + HMA Scalping Strategy

Type of Strategy:

- Scalping

Strategy Overview:

This strategy uses a moving average crossover on the MFI (money flow index), and the Bjorgum MTF MA with the HMA (Hull moving average) setting.

Entry signals occur when the MFI crosses the moving average and price closes above/below the moving average. The trades using this strategy are typically quick scalp trades.

This strategy also uses to 200 MA to trade in the direction of the overall trend.

Strategy Indicators:

- **Bjorgum MTF MA** (by Bjorgum)

  *Change MA type #1 to **HMA** and length of MA #1 to **65**

- **MFI** with a **18 SMA** added on it

  *Change MFI length to 21

- **200 SMA**

Long Entry Conditions:
- Price is above the 200 SMA
- The MFI crosses above the SMA while below 50
- Candle crosses and closes above the HMA
- Candle color changes blue

Long Exit Conditions:
Choose one of the following-
- The MFI crosses below the SMA
- Candle color changes red
- A candle closes below the HMA

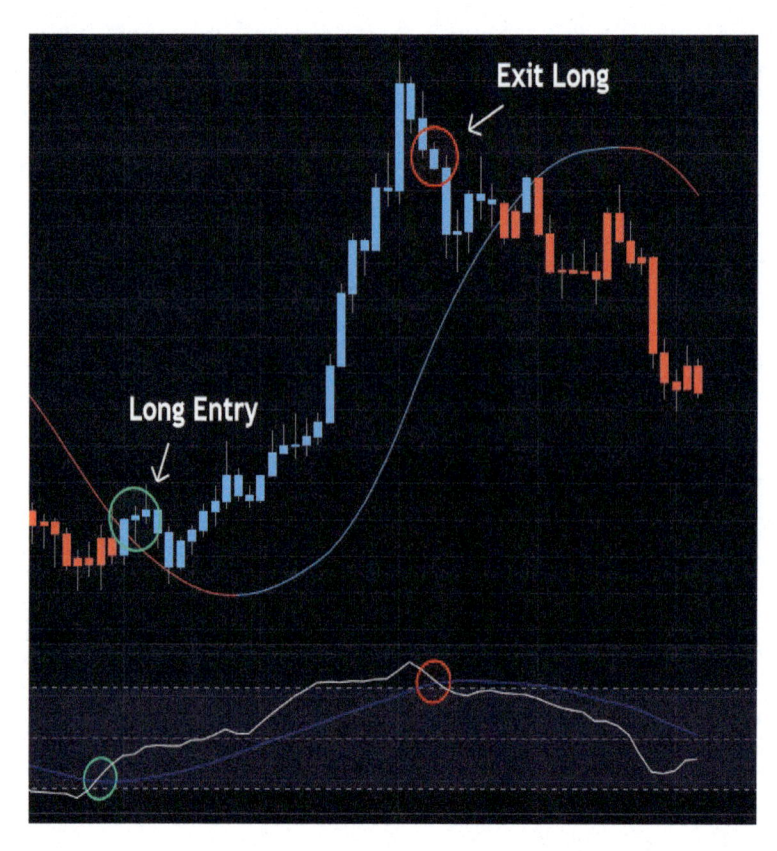

Example of a long entry and exit using this strategy

Short Entry Conditions:
- Price is below the 200 SMA
- The MFI crosses below the SMA while above 50
- Candle crosses and closes below the HMA
- Candle color changes red

Short Exit Conditions:
Choose one of the following-

- The MFI crosses above the SMA
- Candle color changes blue
- A candle closes above the HMA

Strategy #4: BB Reversal Scalping Strategy

Type of Strategy:

- Scalping/mean reversion

Strategy Overview:

This is a mean reversion trading strategy that is designed for scalping in rangebound/sideways market conditions. The breakout/consolidation filter is used to identify and take trades in these conditions.

The Bollinger bands and reversal finder are used for entries and exits.

Strategy Indicators:

- Bollinger band (default settings)
- Reversal finder indicator (by NS91)
- Breakout/Consolidation Filter (by jwammo12)

Long Entry Conditions:

- The breakout/consolidation filter is below 50
- Price is outside or touching the bottom Bollinger band

- A green dot appears under the candle

Long Exit Conditions:
- Price touches or is outside the top Bollinger band
- A red or yellow dot appears above a candle

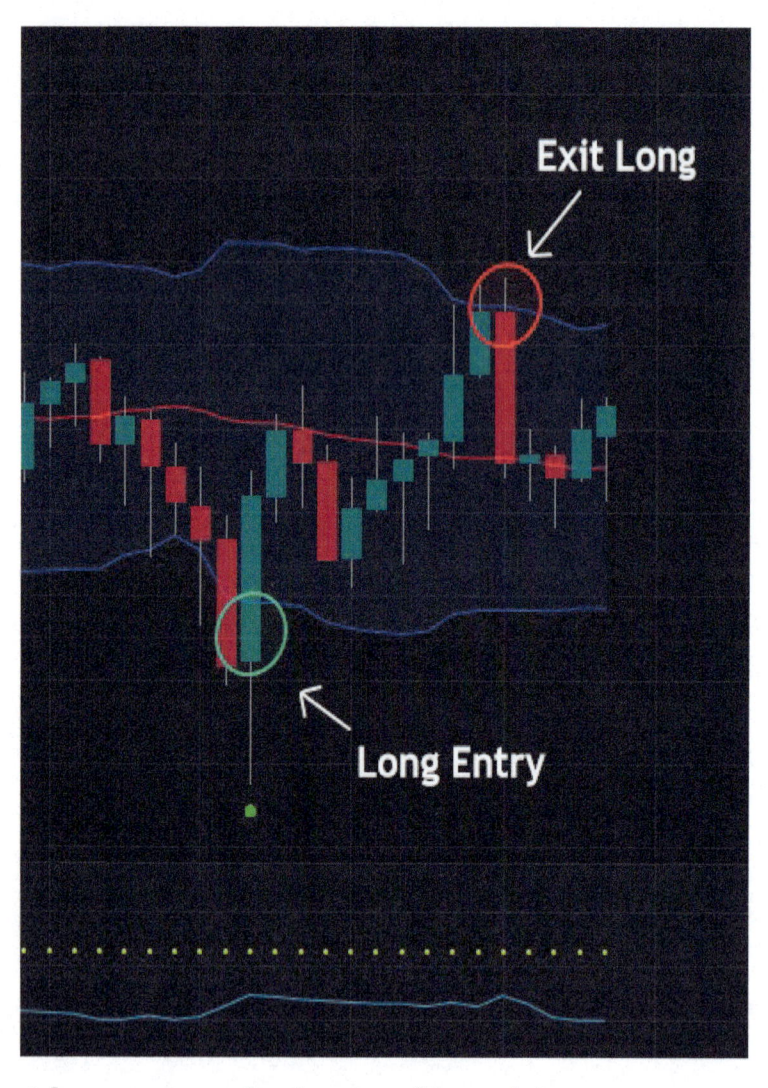

A long entry and exit using this scalping strategy

Short Entry Conditions:
- The breakout/consolidation filter is below 50
- Price is outside or touching the top Bollinger band
- Red dot appears above the candle

Short Exit Conditions:
- Price touches or is outside the bottom Bollinger band
- A green or yellow dot appears below a candle

Strategy #5: Pivot Bands Scalping Strategy

Type of Strategy:

- Scalping/mean reversion

Strategy Overview:

This is a scalping strategy using the CM pivot bands indicator and the Williams %R (the willy) indicators for scalping short term price swings in the market.

When price touches the top or bottom of the CM pivot bands it will likely act as support/resistance levels where price will reverse.

The Williams %R indicator used in this strategy is similar to the RSI. This version of the Williams %R indicator uses a moving average for identifying signals.

This strategy will work the best in sideways/rangebound markets, the ADX is used to filter out trending market conditions.

Strategy Indicators:

- **CM Pivot Bands V1** (By ChrisMoody)

    *Change the length to **20**

- **Williams %R** (by Stuehmer)
- **ADX**

Long Entry Conditions:
- The ADX is below 25
- Candles are closing in the bottom green band
- Enter long when the Williams%R crosses above the MA

Long Exit Conditions:
Choose one of the following-
- Price touches the top red band
- The Williams%R crosses below the MA
- The Williams %R crosses into the overbought zone (-80)

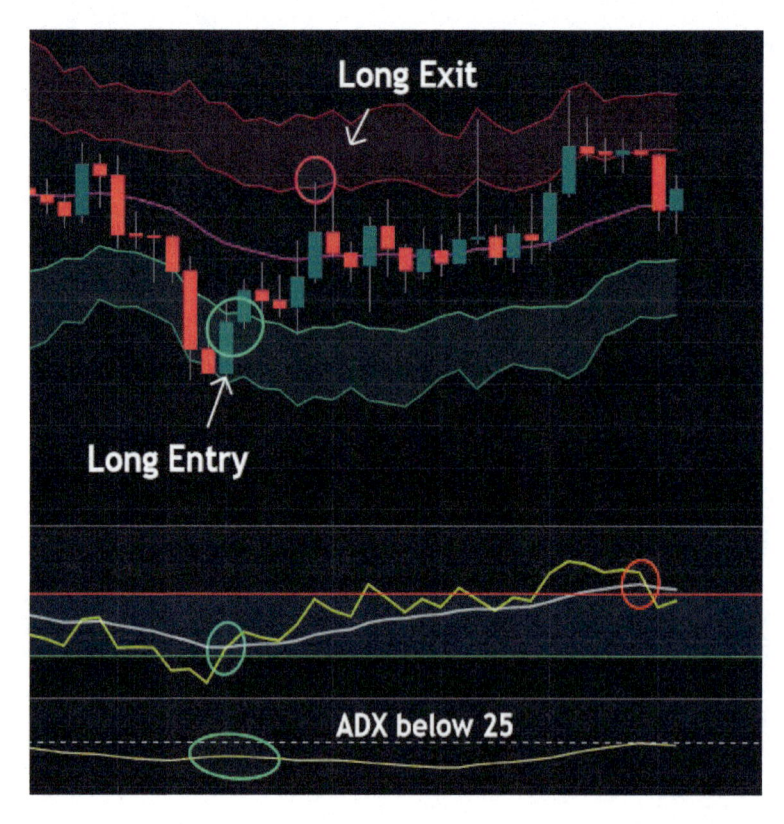

Example of a long entry and exit using this strategy

Short Entry Conditions:
- The ADX is below 25
- Candles are closing in the top red band
- Enter short when the Williams%R crosses below the MA

Short Exit Conditions:
Choose one of the following-
- Price touches the bottom green band
- The Williams%R crosses above the MA
- The Williams %R crosses into the oversold zone (-80)

Strategy #6: RSI and BB Scalping Strategy

Type of Strategy:

- Mean reversion/scalping

Strategy Overview:

This is a mean reversion scalping strategy using the RSI and Bollinger bands to identify high probability entries/exits. These two indicators produce very accurate OB/OS signals in range bound markets.

The ADX is used in this strategy as a filter to identify when a market is in a period of consolidation and moving sideways.

Strategy Indicators:

- **ADX**
- **RSI**

    *Change RSI length to 5

Long Entry Conditions:
- The ADX is below 25
- Price is below or touching the bottom BB
- Enter when the RSI is below 30(oversold) and crosses up out of the oversold zone.

Long Exit Conditions:
Choose one of the following -
- Price touches or crosses above the top BB
- The RSI crosses above 70 (overbought)

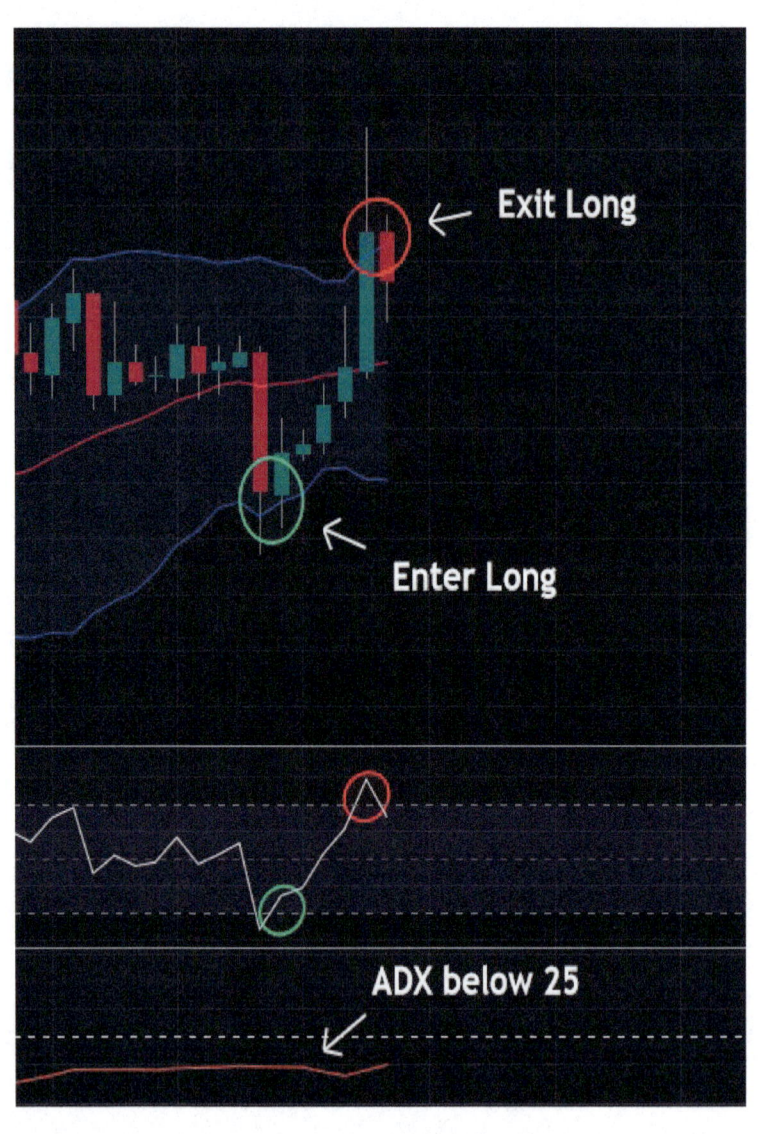

A long entry and exit using this strategy

Short Entry Conditions;

- The ADX is below 25
- Price is above or touching the top BB
- Enter when the RSI is above 70(overbought) and crosses down out of the overbought zone.

Short Exit Conditions:
Choose one of the following -

- Price touches or crosses below the bottom BB
- The RSI crosses below 30 (oversold)

Strategy #7: UT Bot + KDJ

Type of Strategy:

- Can be used for scalping or trend following

Strategy Overview:

This strategy uses the UT Bot Alert indicator for accurately identifying trends, and the KDJ indicator for perfect entries in the trend.

Once you enter the trend, you can decide to ride it out or scalp it for a quicker trade depending on your trading style and preference.

This strategy also uses a 200 SMA to trade in the direction of the overall trend.

Strategy Indicators:

- **UT Bot Alerts** (by QuantNomad)

    *Change settings - Key Value = 3, ATR period = 30

- **L2 KDJ with Whale Pump Detector** (by blackcat 1402)

    *You can turn off the background colors on the KDJ in the settings

- **200 SMA**

Long Entry Conditions:
- Price is above the 200 SMA
- Candle color is green and a buy label appears below a candle
- Enter when a green "B" letter appears on the KDJ, or all three KDJ lines cross up.

Long Exit Conditions:
Choose one of the following-
- A red "S" letter appears on the KDJ
- The three KDJ lines cross down
- Candle color changes to red and a sell label appears above a candle

Example of a long entry and exit signal using this strategy

Short Entry Conditions:

- Price is below the 200 SMA

- Candle color is red and a sell label appears above a candle

- Enter when a red "S" letter appears on the KDJ, or all three KDJ lines cross down.

Short Exit Conditions:

Choose one of the following-

- A green "B" letter appears on the KDJ

- The three KDJ lines cross down

- Candle color changes to red and a sell label appears above a candle

Printed in Great Britain
by Amazon